HOW TO BE A
DYNAMITE TRUSTEE

Book One Of A Four Part Series

BY

A. JEANNE EMANUEL, ATTORNEY AT LAW
THOMAS A. EMANUEL, PROFESSIONAL FIDUCIARY

COPYRIGHT

This book can be located using the following International Standard Book Numbers (ISBN):

ISBN-13:
978-1497588585

ISBN-10:
1497588588

ACKNOWLEDGEMENTS

We would like to express our profound gratitude for the thousands of clients who have asked us questions which led to our realization that Trustors and their Trustees need the information we have tried to supply in this series. We appreciate all of them more than we know how to express. We hope that you, our reader, will feel that they have asked many of the same questions you have, and more importantly that if you are confident in our answers that you will pass on the information to those of your friends and family similarly situated.

ABOUT THE AUTHORS

JEANNE EMANUEL is an estate planning attorney. She has over 40 years of experience, the last 32 solely in the area of estate planning. She graduated with honors from Western State University College of Law and is now a nationally and internationally known estate planner, speaker and author. Jeanne is also a gifted artist who loves to paint birds, wildlife and California beach scenes. She is happiest when traveling and exploring with her husband anywhere in the world.

Thomas Emanuel acts as a professional fiduciary and trustee for selected estates and has worked in the estate planning and trust administration field for more than 25 years. He holds a Master's degree from Georgetown University. Tom is an accomplished writer and speaker. He is a voracious reader and loves to travel with his wife.

The Emanuels make their home in northern Baja California, Mexico. This book is their fourth collaboration as authors, but the first they have produced as a series because of the extensive nature of the topic.

To learn more about their books look for their names as authors on Amazon and Kindle. You can contact them by writing to TJEPUBLISHING@gmail.com.

The authors would greatly appreciate it if you would write a review of this book on Amazon.com. Help get this book in the hands of people who need it. Thank you.

DISCLAIMER

The information, ideas, and suggestions in this book are not intended to render legal advice. Before following any suggestions contained in this book, you should consult your personal attorney. Neither the authors nor the publisher shall be liable or responsible in any way for any loss or damage allegedly arising as a consequence of your use or application of any information or suggestions in this book.

TABLE OF CONTENTS
TOPICS COVERED

CHAPTER THREE: THE SUCCESSOR TRUSTEE

PURPOSE OF THIS BOOK

Our intent in this series is to provide our readers with valuable, comprehensive information on the organization of trusts, the legal and ethical responsibilities of the Trustee and any Successor Trustee, and ways to avoid the numerous pitfalls hidden from the uninitiated.

First of all we recognize a crucial fact. Almost everyone experiences the duties of a Trustee as a once in a life time event. That is because, unless you are a professional fiduciary, you will not have had occasion to work in this capacity before. This means that you are liable to make mistakes - sometimes very serious ones - because of lack of experience in these matters.

It could take a very considerable period of time to become educated in this area if you were flying solo. That is why this series is so valuable to you. How do you know when you have reached the right level of competence? How do you know if you have learned all you need to know?

That is where this series can provide you both important answers and psychological relief. You can move forward with confidence, knowing that you have all the right questions covered and you have received the correct answers from true professionals.

So let me congratulate you. You have done the right thing, made a wise choice in purchasing this book.

We have tried to make a, perhaps dull, subject more palatable by a question and answer format. We are taking it from your point of view. You want to know what you need to know and you want to be assured that you are asking all the right questions. Tom Emanuel will be asking the questions from your point of view. Jeanne Emanuel will be providing the answers and the explanations based on her many years of advising thousands of clients in the field of estate planning.

You will get the answers you need and you can be assured that the subject is covered very thoroughly.

We hope you not only benefit from this book but actually enjoy learning the very important things you need to know about how to be a proud, professional and competent Trustee or Successor Trustee.

CHAPTER ONE

ESTATE PLANNING AND PROBATE

Everyone involved with a revocable living trust must know the facts explored in this chapter. Some of them are generally known by the public but are often not accurately stated. Some of them are bit less part of common knowledge. If you have a trust, are planning on getting a trust, or even if you think you don't need a trust this is pertinent information to have at your disposal.

Tom: Welcome to this opportunity to learn what you need to know now that you have been named a Trustee. Your attorney is A. Jeanne Emanuel. Jeanne has been an Estate Planning Attorney for 32 years. During this period, Jeanne has worked with thousands of people both in planning their estates, and guiding Successor Trustees of Revocable Living Trusts. In this book we are going to be discussing how to administer and distribute a small trust estate of less than the Federal Estate Tax limit, which at the present time is any estate of less than $5,000,000. Jeanne will give us instructions as to exactly what to do, and when to do it. As a beginning I will ask Jeanne to explain what estate planning is all about? What is a Revocable Living Trust? How is it used? How does a person become a Trustee in the first place? Jeanne, please tell us what is estate planning all about, and why should people do it?

Jeanne: Thank you very much. I'm excited to be able to help. I know from experience that there are a lot of people looking for the answers to the questions you are going to ask me. Now to answer you first question, what is estate planning? It is simply a way by which you can control the distribution of your material assets after your death, or during your lifetime, if you happen to be incapacitated. It means different things to each person, depending on their particular set of circumstances, goals and objectives.

Tom: I imagine their age bracket and the size of estate would have a lot to do with it.

Jeanne: That's right. The planning is very different for, say, a very young couple with small children, as opposed to a widow in her seventies, who has grown children and grandchildren. My job is to help a client define what those goals are, and then to devise an estate plan to effectively achieve them.

Tom: So the initial planning is important, isn't it?

Jeanne: Yes. However, in each case there are certain common goals that should be planned for and achieved. Everyone wants to preserve as much of the estate as possible from the high costs of the probate system, and eliminate any inheritance tax as much as possible. It seems to me, that before we get into the administration of a Revocable Living Trust, we should first know how the trust works, and how it avoids probate.

Tom: So just what is probate?

Jeanne: I like to tell my clients that each State has a plan for transferring the assets of a deceased person. This means, that if a person does not have a plan for themselves, the State has one for them. It's called probate. It is a court procedure that enables the dead person's assets to be transferred to their heirs, based on a Will, expressing their wishes, or by intestate succession, meaning without a Will. Naturally, because there is a court procedure involved, it is complicated, requires the services of an attorney, and it's usually very time consuming.

Tom: You mean that even if I have a Will, my estate will have to go to probate?

Jeanne: Yes. A Will is designed to go through probate, because probate is the process of proving up a Will. Until it is submitted to the probate court for approval and administration it has no force and effect at all. Another misconception people have is, that if the estate is less than the Federal Inheritance Tax limit (currently $5,000,000), they don't have to go to probate. That is simply not true.

Tom: I thought it was true! What is the $5,000,000 number then?

Jeanne: That's the amount of a net estate which is not subject to Federal Inheritance Tax. But the amount of money which will put your estate into probate is different. It also varies by State. For example, in Nebraska the maximum amount that a deceased person can have is $10,000 in gross assets, without being subject to formal probate. In California it's $100,000.

Tom: Well, I know that I don't want my estate to go to probate, if I can avoid it. I'd rather have my family have all the money, and save them the grief as well. I have heard that there are some ways to avoid probate. Is that true?

Jeanne: Yes. Any property that has a designated beneficiary, like an insurance policy, or property held in joint tenancy, or tenancy by the entirety with the right of survivorship, is not subject to probate. The recipient is already identified and the court's assistance is not needed.

Tom: But isn't the recipient already identified in a Will?

Jeanne: Yes, but there are still serious questions that the court must decide. Is it the final Will executed by the person? Was it made freely, and in accordance with the requirements for a valid Will under the laws of that State. Are there objections from possible heirs? The court must investigate all these and many other questions.

Tom: I have heard that going through probate is not only an emotionally devastating experience for the family, but that it is extremely costly to the estate as well.

Jeanne: Oh, it can be absolutely devastating! Especially to small estates! Ten percent of the gross estate is not an unusual cost. Ten percent can be a very large number in relation to the size of the estate.

Tom: What do you mean?

Jeanne: Well, if the total estate is $250,000 gross and probate takes ten percent, or $25,000, that leaves only $225,000, not including paying any debts. That looks like a much bigger bite to the heirs than if the estate were $2,000,000 leaving a net of $1,800,000.

Tom: $1,800,000 is still a lot of money! I never thought of it that way. But I see what you mean. It may be even more important for people with smaller estates to plan in this area, than for those with substantial assets.

Jeanne: Exactly! But unfortunately everyone is convinced of just the opposite. They think, "Oh I don't have much so it doesn't really matter". Actually, it matters a great deal.

Tom: How are probate fees calculated? And why are they so expensive?

Jeanne: In many States, the fees charged are dictated by statute for both the executor and the attorney. They are so expensive because they are based on the gross estate, not the net (which is after loans and all other debts are satisfied). This means that it is possible to pay more in probate fees on a piece of property than the property is worth. On top of these statutory fees the attorney and the executor can charge additional fees for extraordinary services. There are often many services that must be done which are not designated in the statute.

Tom: Does it really take at least a year or more to go through probate? I imagine that could really add to the expense.

Jeanne: It depends on the jurisdiction. But a year is not uncommon and in fact it can often be much longer.

Tom: Is the living trust a good way to avoid probate and still keep control of your property?

Jeanne: Yes, the living trust is the very best way to avoid probate, since it leaves the Trustor in complete control of his property, and it does not subject it to the liabilities of other people, which is a major drawback in using joint tenancy as an estate planning method. Everyone who owns real estate, stocks or bonds needs the revocable living trust as their basic planning tool.

15

This very flexible document makes several common and essential goals in estate planning happen.

CHAPTER TWO: TRUST STRUCTURE

In this chapter the question and answer format continues while Tom and Jeanne discuss the structure of a revocable living trust and the various benefits of creating one.

Tom: Jeanne this material has been very informative so far, but now I would like to ask you some questions about the trust itself and why it is a good idea to create one. First, what is so great about a revocable living trust?

Jeanne: Well, a revocable living trust is terrific because, first, it avoids probate altogether. Second, it eliminates, or at least minimizes, death taxes. Third, it makes attacks on the estate by disgruntled heirs very difficult or impossible. That alone can be a very critical factor. Fourth, the trustor has complete control over the estate during his lifetime and over its distribution after his death. Fifth, it keeps the affairs of the estate completely private. The trust is not recorded or filed as a public document. Sixth, it protects the trustors from conservatorship, if they should be come incapacitated. The successor trustee can just step into their shoes. And lastly, the trustor appoints the successor trustee, who takes over for them when their gone. It is a GREAT document.

Tom: In a nutshell then, people who utilize the living trust in their estate planning can keep control of their own estate even after they die, while saving thousands of dollars, which will go to their loved ones instead of attorneys and the court system.

Jeanne: Yes! Isn't it wonderful? People think trusts are just for rich people, or at least people with larger estates. But as we have just discovered, that is just not true.

Tom: But I've had people tell me that their attorney has advised them against having a trust, saying that their estate didn't warrant it because it was under the Federal Inheritance Tax limit. What about that?

Jeanne: Yes, I've heard the same thing, and in some limited situations that may be true. But not to cast aspersions on the legal profession, I should point out that probate has traditionally been part of the retirement plan for many attorneys. They make a lot more money probating the estate than in creating a living trust.

Tom: I can see how that might be an influencing factor.

Jeanne: In some cases it could be that the attorney is not well versed in the merits of the living trust. In my opinion, people who have an estate in excess of the State's threshold for probate would be well advised to look at the advantages of such planning. It is usually a case of choosing to pay a little for planning now, or having the estate pay a lot more in fees later.

Tom: What does it cost to have a living trust created?

Jeanne: It depends a lot on how much transfer work needs to be done, the complexity of the distribution and tax planning, whether the trustor is married or not, and whether any special needs have to be covered by specialized provisions in the trust.

18

But a good credible job can be done for most average estates for a fee which is considerably less than just the minimum cost of probate.

Tom: So compared to probate a trust is a bargain.

Jeanne: That is totally true. When you add in possible inheritance tax savings, and remember that many States have such taxes as well, then the trust becomes the best bargain in town.

Tom: Well, once you create a trust, is that the end of the story? Is that all you have to do?

Jeanne: No. To make the trust effective you must transfer all of your assets to the trust. The trust must have legal title to your assets when you die. The trustee is the one who has the right to take action on these assets. While you are alive you own the trust and you are your own trustee, unless you are legally incapacitated. When your successor trustee takes control of the trust after you die, there will be no necessity to go to court to have the titles transferred, and thus probate is avoided. This is why it is so vital that the trustor(s) take the time and make the effort to make sure that all their property belongs to the trust.

Tom: So the trust owns everything and a trust cannot die. Therefore, no probate is needed. But what happens if not all of the property gets transferred to the trust?

Jeanne: Good question! There should always be two documents that back up the trust. A Pour-Over Will, names the trust as the sole beneficiary of the estate. It is called that because the Will pours everything that is not in the trust already over into the trust. Also the Durable Power of Attorney Over Assets names an agent who can transfer property to the trust, if necessary. I always like to name the successor trustee as both the personal representative (in the Will) and the agent (for the Durable Power) in these documents. Then if property is inadvertently left out of the trust, the successor trustee can transfer it to the trust.

Tom: Okay. Now, when a trust is properly funded and the last trustor dies, just what happens?

Jeanne: Well, the successor trustee steps into the shoes of the deceased trustor and takes over.

CHAPTER THREE: THE SUCCESSOR TRUSTEE

This chapter provides information about the creation of a Successor Trustee, his authority, the types of people who are eligible to be a Successor Trustee, and his fees, if any. Also we will briefly touch on the enforcement of the trust. Tom continues with the questioning.

Tom: You know, I think we need to define some terms here. What do you mean by a successor trustee?

Jeanne: Oh, that's easy! First, let's understand the structure of the living trust. When a trust is created it has three positions which must be filled. The first is the trustor(s), the person or persons who create the trust and can modify or revoke it. The second is the trustee, the person who manages the assets owned by the trust. And the third is the beneficiary or beneficiaries of the trust, the person(s) who receive the benefits of those assets. All three positions can be, and often are, occupied by the same person or persons, such as a married couple. Now, to answer your question, the successor trustee is the person named by the trustor to take the place of the original trustee once that position is vacated.

Tom: I'm glad you clarified that. But how does a person get the authority to act as a successor trustee?

Jeanne: There are three ways this happens. But first I must re-emphasize that this applies to the small estates under the Federal Inheritance Tax limit. Trusts requiring tax avoidance planning and very complicated distributions will be handled under a different book.

Tom: Okay, so in that context, what are the three ways?

Jeanne: Let's take the typical married couple with a trust. The first spouse dies and the other spouse continues as the trustee. This is not a successor trustee because the remaining spouse was already a trustee. When the second spouse dies, the successor trustee named in the trust takes over. Another way for a successor trustee to be activated is by resignation of the prior trustee, who is not also the trustor and initial trustee. The third way is by appointment. The appointment can be by a court of competent jurisdiction or by the beneficiaries of the trust themselves.

Tom: Got it! Now, let's explore the death, resignation, or incapacity of the initial trustee.

Jeanne: Good choice. That is the most common form of acquiring authority. But I have a suggestion. I think we should handle the least common methods first. Then we can go more extensively into what usually happens.

Tom: Okay. That's fine.

Jeanne: The least common way of acquiring trustee authority is by appointment of the court. Let's assume the trust names only one successor trustee. The last trustor dies and so does the trustee. The named successor is unavailable. The trust does not provide a method of naming a new trustee.

Tom: Wait a minute! I thought the court system did not need to be involved at all.

Jeanne: Generally, that's true, especially if the trust is well drafted and takes care of all foreseeable contingencies. However, there are some limited instances where the Trustee will want direction from the court, or where, in a case like this, the trust agreement is silent or ambiguous in its terms. In other words, this trust did not give the beneficiaries the authority to name a new trustee. Then the beneficiaries will have to file a petition to have a new trustee appointed. This is pretty rare, but it does point out how important it is that an alternate successor trustee be named. That avoids this kind of situation.

Tom: Good. You mentioned something about resignation of a prior trustee, who is not also the trustor and initial trustee.

Jeanne: Yes. This is a situation where the first named successor trustee is unable to fulfill his or her obligation. He will sign a formal resignation as the trustee, which will name the next designated person as successor. This is not an uncommon experience.

Tom: Really! Can you elaborate?

Jeanne: Sure. Sometimes a person is ill, or just cannot do it because of their location or schedule. I had a recent client who was already the on-going trustee of her uncle's estate which had been in probate for two years because some of his property was not in the trust. This required probate of the property outside the trust. So when her sister died naming her as trustee, she had to resign. She was sad about it but she just could not handle it properly, so she signed a formal letter of resignation and the other named trustee took over.

Tom: Does that cover the least common cases?

Jeanne: Yes. Now let's handle the more usual or ordinary cases. The last trustor dies, becomes incompetent, or resigns as initial trustee. Sometimes the trustor reaches an age where, even though they are perfectly able to continue to manage their own affairs, they just don't want to bother. At that point they often name someone as co-trustee to help them.

Tom: That's smart. Much better than giving somebody access to your money without restraint.

Jeanne: In a very common case, however, the trustor becomes incompetent through old age or senility and is no longer able to handle his own affairs.

Tom: Does the successor trustee just decide that the trustor has become incompetent, and takes over, or is other proof required?

Jeanne: The successor trustee can't just take over, but must have the family doctor verify the trustor's disability. Often the verification must be made by two independent doctors. This avoids a situation where someone could just wrongfully take over the trustor's property. It also avoids the necessity of going to court to have a judge appoint a conservator over the person. That would require periodic accounting from the conservator to the court. In addition, it saves the estate the attorney fees and court costs.

Tom: Once the successor has the doctors' verification, how does he take over?

Jeanne: This document and the trust agreement allows the successor access to bank accounts, gives him authority to sell property, and gives him ability to administer the estate and exercise all the powers provided for in the trust.

Tom: Then the successor trustee can do anything he wants with the estate.

Jeanne: No. The trustor still remains as the beneficiary of the trust. The successor must use the trust assets only for the benefit of the trustor. He is subject to all the duties owed by a trustee to a beneficiary.

Tom: Yeah, that's good. But it's still the death of the last trustor that is the most common method of becoming the successor trustee, right?

Jeanne: That's exactly right. When the last trustor dies, the successor trustee takes over the affairs of the trust. This is automatic. No permission is required from the court or anyone else.

Tom: Who can be a successor trustee, just anybody?

Jeanne: As long as they are competent, of legal age to sign contracts, of sound mind, and meet the criteria used by the trustor, they can serve as trustee. But choosing the successor trustee should not be taken lightly. It must be someone who can handle this responsibility. It should also be someone who will not cause a problem in the family.

Tom: What do you mean by that?

Jeanne: Most of the time, especially with small estates, the successor trustee will be one of the children. This can sometimes cause dissention within the family if the other children have no respect for, feel resentment of the successor, or have some other unresolved problems with the successor.

Tom: I bet that is something to think about! Families can get into a lot of emotional turmoil when money is involved.

Jeanne: Or sometimes it isn't even the money. It's a control issue. This is something that should be considered, especially where there is a second marriage with children from different marriages. In some of these cases it is better to use an unrelated third party as the successor.

Tom: Isn't that expensive. I thought only banks and trust companies did that sort of thing. Plus, they only want bigger estates, right?

Jeanne: Not necessarily. Some of them take estates as small as $250,000. There are also private fiduciaries who will act as trustee. Their fees are typically less, and they can be more personally involved. Lack of personal contact and understanding are usually the most serious objections to naming a corporate trustee.

Tom: I would want to be very careful about appointing someone I didn't know. What if they just ripped off the estate?

Jeanne: You would certainly want references before you appointed such a person, and the trust document should provide that such a person be bonded to protect against that type of conduct. But there are some very reputable professionals available, and they should not be overlooked as a potential successor trustee where family is not appropriate.

Tom: What about naming the attorney who drafts the trust as the trustee?

Jeanne: Most attorneys decline the appointment as trustee feeling that there is an inherent conflict of interest. In some States (I know California is one) the attorney is prohibited from serving as the trustee.

Tom: Probably not a good idea, then. How much are the fees for the trustee? And are friends or family entitled to them too?

Jeanne: The trustee is entitled to reasonable fees no matter who they are. They devote time and effort to the job and they often fully deserve them. Usually, they receive about one percent of the total value of the estate per year. But this can range higher depending on the length of time the trust is to exist and the complexity of the trust assets managed. If they perform extraordinary services for the trust, they should be compensated for them.

Tom: What would be considered extraordinary services?

Jeanne: Here's an example. I had a client who had to sell trust property located over 100 miles from her home. She made several trips to the property, removed and sold all the personal effects of the decedent, engaged a realtor, and went through escrow in a distant city. These were extraordinary services in addition to her normal duties as trustee.

Tom: So what are the normal duties of a trustee?

Jeanne: That requires an extensive discussion which we cover in the in the next couple of chapters clarifying the duties of a successor trustee. But here I would like to point out that most successors are the children of the trustors. All they typically have to do is distribute the assets of the estate and file the final tax return. Under these conditions they often waive any fee, especially if they are also one of the beneficiaries.

Tom: Okay. Let's assume that my parents had a trust and they have both died. I am named as the successor trustee. What is the first thing I have to do?

Jeanne: This may seem very obvious, but people often don't do the obvious. **READ THE TRUST DOCUMENT!**

Tom: Good point!

Jeanne: The first thing you want to find out is what you are expected to do under the terms of the trust. Are you going to do an immediate distribution of the assets to the beneficiaries, including yourself? Are there some assets which will continue to be held in trust for a period of time?

Tom: Wait. I thought the assets are always fully distributed.

Jeanne: No. There are many cases where beneficiaries are entitled to a portion of the estate but they are not to receive them until some criteria are met. They may have to reach a certain age, they might have to graduate from college, and they might not get a lump sum until the trustee determines that they are responsible enough to handle it.

Tom: Does that mean they don't get anything from the trust until then?

Jeanne: That could be the case. But usually the trust provides that the trustee can distribute both income and principal for the benefit of the beneficiary for certain types of needs. The costs of education, living expenses, or health care are examples of needs where distribution is allowed. The trustee is typically given broad discretion to determine what should be done in this respect.

Tom: Speaking of that, how is a trust enforced? You said a trust is entirely private, not filed with the court. Who makes sure that the trustee does what he is told to do?

Jeanne: The beneficiaries enforce the trust. Obviously, this presents some problems when the beneficiary does not know he or she has been named, or is a minor, or is incompetent. These issues are addressed in another chapter of the book. But as to what can be expected of a successor trustee, it all depends on the terms of the trust and on the types of beneficiaries involved.

Tom: This is an eye opener! I didn't realize this subject was so complicated. Are you sure that this is something that most successor trustees can handle by themselves?

Jeanne: For the most part, yes. It really just takes a little common sense. At times guidance from an estate planning attorney can be very useful. If the trustee is willing to do all the leg work and only looks to the lawyer for guidance as needed, it need not be too expensive.

CHAPTER FOUR: WHAT HAVE WE LEARNED?

This chapter contains a summary and review of the contents of this book.

Tom: Now, let's recall what we have learned. Estate planning is the setting out of the goals people have for the transfer of their estate after they die.

Jeanne: Very good! Keep going.

Tom: The revocable living trust is the most important and popular tool utilized to accomplish these goals for people with both large and small estates. It's very inexpensive when compared to the costs of probate and taxes.

Jeanne: Correct.

Tom: The way the trust works is that, if the trustor has transferred all of the estate assets to the trust, it legally owns everything when the trustor dies. Therefore, there is no need for the expense and aggravation of probate.

Jeanne: Exactly. The person named by the trustor, as the successor trustee, simply takes over and handles the affairs of the estate. Do you remember the three positions in the trust?

Tom: Yep. The trustor creates the trust, names the successor trustee and tells him what to do. The original trustee manages the property owned by the trust. This is usually the same person as the trustor. And the last position is that of beneficiary who receives the benefits of the trust assets. There again they are usually the same person(s) as the trustor(s), until the trustor dies.

Jeanne: We also know that the complexity of what the successor trustee has to do depends upon who the beneficiaries are. Some of the trustee's duties can go on for many years and can be numerous. Now we have a great basis for exploring the duties of the trustee, the various types of trusts, and the practical aspects of actually performing trustee duties.

Tom: Thank you, Jeanne. This has been very enlightening and important information. We look forward to other topics in this area to explore as thoroughly and interestingly as you have tackled this one.

We also want to thank you, our reader. If you enjoyed this book we urge you to read the other three books in this series. We also would really appreciate it if you would do a review of this book on Amazon, it will help to get it in the hands of people who really need the information.

The second book concentrates on the responsibilities and duties of the trustee. The third book speaks to the various different types of trusts and continues the discussion on trustee duties. And the fourth book explains exactly what the actual steps are when the trustee undertakes his duties. All of this information, and the proper way to apply it, is required in order to make a person into a competent, nay dynamite, trustee.

If you want to contact the authors please do so at TJEPUBLISHING@GMAIL.COM.

Thank you again for your determination to do your job as a trustee to the best of your ability.

APPENDIX I: RESOURCES

OTHER BOOKS BY THE AUTHORS:

HOW TO BE A DYNAMITE TRUSTEE: BOOK ONE OF A FOUR PART SERIES

HOW TO BE A DYNAMITE TRUSTEE: BOOK TWO POWERS OF THE TRUSTEE

HOW TO BE A DYNAMITE TRUSTEE: BOOK THREE ON GOING TRUSTS

HOW TO BE A DYNAMITE TRUSTEE: BOOK FOUR PRACTICAL MATTERS

THE PERFECT LAST IMPRESSION: WILLS, TRUSTS, AND ESTATE PLANS FOR HAPPY HEIRS

PRIVACY, MONEY, AND IDENTITY PROTECTION BY BANKING IN BELIZE

RECOMMENDED BOOKS BY OTHER AUTHORS:

ESTATE and TRUST ADMINSTRATION FOR DUMMIES by Margaret Atkins Monroe

THE EVERYTHING EXECUTOR and TRUST BOOK: A STEP-BY-STEP GUIDE TO ESTATE and TRUST ADMINISTRATION by Douglas D. Wilson

THE TRUSTEE'S LEGAL COMPANION: A STEP-BY-STEP GUIDE TO ADMINISTERING A LIVING TRUST by Carol Elias, Attorney Zolla

THE EXECUTOR'S GUIDE: SETTLING A LOVED ONE'S ESTATE OR TRUST by Mary Randolph, J. D.

HOW TO SETTLE AN ESTATE by Charles K. Plotnick and Stephen R. Leimberg

THE COMPLETE GUIDE TO TRUST AND ESTATE MANAGEMENT: WHAT YOU NEED TO KNOW ABOUT BEING A TRUSTEE OR AN EXECUTOR by Linda C. Ashar

Note: All of these books are available on Amazon or Kindle.

***** **THE END** *****